The Book of the Rosary

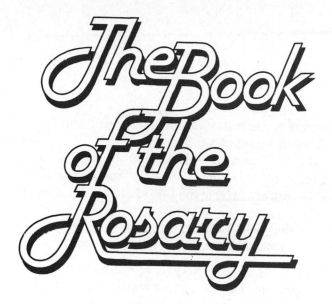

The Book of the Rosary

By John Joseph Cardinal Carberry
Former Archbishop of Saint Louis

Illustrations by James E. McIlrath

Our Sunday Visitor, Inc.

Dedication

To the Immaculate Heart of Mary
Our Lady of Fatima
The Queen of Peace

Contents

Illustrations

Foreword

During Vatican Council II, because of media reports which were confusing and misleading, there developed a coolness in general to devotion to Our Lady, and in particular to the Rosary. The Fathers of the Council never intended this. In fact, in the Eighth Chapter of the Constitution on the Church the perennial and sacred teaching on Mary is clearly and strongly expressed. This lack of devotion to Mary was noticeable, and a source of disappointment. During the decade of the '50s it had been altogether different. That period was known as the "Era of Mary" because she was so beloved and extolled. Pope Pius XII was, indeed, a devotee of Mary. But by the mid-'60s the devotion had decidedly waned.

Under the succeeding pontiffs, however, efforts were made to counteract this apparent indifference to the Mother of God. More and more Mary was spoken of, and the Message of Our Lady of Fatima began to be heard in loud tones. Pope John Paul II, whose episcopal motto is *Totus Tuus* ("I Am All Thine"), attributed his recovery from wounds of attempted assassination to the intercession of Mary. On May 13, 1982, he made a thanksgiving visit to Fatima for his life having been spared. At the same time, in a solemn manner in accordance with Mary's wishes, he consecrated the world and Russia to her Immaculate Heart, in spiritual union with all the bishops of the world.

From then on revival of love for Mary and her Rosary took on a noticeable renewal. It was almost like the lighting of a torch of love. Many dioceses in this country, under the leadership of their bishops, were consecrated to the Immaculate Heart of Mary after the manner of the consecration made by Pope John Paul II. He, indeed, is truly a Marian pontiff, one who speaks of her with filial affection in almost every discourse.

A new era of love and devotion to Mary and her Rosary seems to be dawning. The faithful appear to be seeking more knowledge about Our Lady and her beloved Rosary.

THE BOOK OF THE ROSARY, please God, is a response to this blessed renewal. It touches many facets of the Rosary and its mysteries. In the meditations proposed, specific topics are selected in each decade and a scriptural passage is cited for contemplation. Further, a glance through the material contained in *THE BOOK OF THE ROSARY* reveals vistas which may strengthen love for the Rosary.

Mary, loving Mother as she is, never seeks herself but wishes to lead souls to Jesus, her Divine Son. His life and teachings are the basis and the golden fabric of the Rosary. Through the pages of *THE BOOK OF THE ROSARY* it is prayerfully expected that an even greater love for Mary and her Rosary will flourish in the hearts of all.

OUR LADY OF THE ROSARY OF FATIMA, PRAY FOR US.

I

The Meaning
and Value
of the Rosary

The Meaning and Value of the Rosary

The sentiments of the Holy See concerning the Most Holy Rosary are truly echoed in the words of Pope John Paul II: "The Rosary is my favorite prayer. A marvelous prayer. Marvelous in its simplicity and depth. . . . I cordially exhort everyone to recite it" (*L'Osservatore Romano*, October 26, 1981, p. 6).

For centuries the successors of Peter have expressed their admiration for the Rosary and have repeatedly exhorted the faithful to its prayerful recitation. Pope Pius XII explicitly declared: "The Apostolic See urgently recommends the recitation of the Rosary" (*Apostolic Constitution on the Dogma of the Assumption*, November 1, 1950).

The attitude of the Popes toward the Rosary is well summarized by Paul VI: "On many occasions [our predecessors] have recommended the frequent recitation of the Rosary; they have encouraged its diffusion, explained its nature, recognized its suitability for fostering contemplative prayer, prayer of both praise and petition, and recalled its intrinsic effectiveness for promoting Christian life and apostolic commitment" (Apostolic Exhortation, *On Devotion to the Blessed Virgin Mary*, February 2, 1974, No. 42).

It can truly be said that of all exercises of piety, no other has received such praise and encouragement by the magisterium of the Church.

Surely, such forceful, continual papal teaching is sufficient reason for the faithful to recite the Rosary. But it would be well to ask why the Church gives such strong encouragement to pray the decades of the Rosary and why Pope after Pope recalls to the flock of Christ the beauty of the Rosary.

The answer is not difficult to find. The ultimate foundation of the Church's love for the Rosary is her intense love for the Word of God.

Vatican II's Constitution on Divine Revelation states: "The Church has always venerated the divine Scriptures just as she venerates the body of the Lord. . . ." The Rosary has been a favored means of providing easy access to the Sacred Scriptures, so urged by the Council. For the Rosary is "the compendium of the entire Gospel," as Pope Pius XII, Pope Paul VI and Pope John Paul II have explicitly pointed out. The Rosary is, according to the magisterium, primarily "a Gospel prayer . . . drawing from the Gospel the presentation of the mysteries and its main formulas" (Paul VI, *On Devotion to the Blessed Virgin Mary*, No. 44).

With Our Blessed Mother, and under her maternal influence, one contemplates through the Rosary the great mysteries of God's love as revealed to us in the inspired Scriptures. What better way to integrate the prayerful reading of the Word of God, to absorb its truth and power, than by the contemplative *telling of the beads*? Through the heart of His Mother, our hearts enter into living communion with Jesus, in His joyful, sorrowful and glorious mysteries.

Mary is the woman "who hears the word of God and keeps it" (see Lk 11:28). Her Rosary creates the atmosphere charged with the power of the Spirit so that, like her, the faithful may be penetrated with the awesome beauty of God's love as revealed in His Word.

When the Church, therefore, so constantly pleads with us to pray the Rosary, she is calling us to be like Mary "pondering in our hearts" (see Lk 2:19) the Gospel mysteries of the Life, Death and Resurrection of Our Savior. The Rosary impels us to pray the Scriptures more fervently and more frequently. It is nothing less than the contemplative celebration of God's joyful, suffering, glorious Word.

Since the Rosary is a "Gospel prayer, centered on the mystery of the redemptive Incarnation," it is an "unceasing praise of Christ" (*On Devotion to the Blessed Virgin Mary*, No. 46). Contemplation of the mysteries of the Lord is the soul of the Rosary. Therefore, its recitation does not, as Paul VI clearly points out, go counter "to the warning of Christ: 'And in praying do not heap up empty phrases as the Gentiles do; for they think that they will be heard for their many words' (Mt 6:7). By its nature, the recitation of the Rosary calls for a quiet rhythm and a lingering pace, helping the individual to meditate on the mysteries of the Lord's life as seen through the

17

eyes of her who was closest to the Lord. In this way the unfathomable riches of these mysteries are unfolded" (*On Devotion to the Blessed Virgin*, No. 47).

The Church so strongly promotes this Marian devotion for another fundamental reason: she must be faithful to the Scriptures which tell us that all generations will call Mary the blessed one (see Lk 1:48). The Marian Rosary is a practical and efficacious way of recognizing Mary's role in salvation history, one of the most beautiful ways of showing loving devotion to her.

The Church constantly explains that authentic devotion to Mary — so beautifully exemplified by the Rosary — is praise of her Son. As St. Louis de Montfort wrote centuries ago: "If then we are establishing sound devotion to Our Blessed Lady, it is only in order to establish devotion to Our Lord more perfectly by providing a smooth but certain way of reaching Jesus Christ. If devotion to Our Lady distracted us from Our Lord, we would have to reject it as an illusion of the devil. But this is far from being the case . . . it is a way of entering into Jesus more perfectly, of loving him more tenderly and of serving him more faithfully" (*True Devotion to the Blessed Virgin*, No.

62). The truth of this strong statement is surely evident in the most widespread of all Marian devotions, the Most Holy Rosary.

There is yet another reason why the supreme pontiffs constantly recommend the Rosary to the entire Church. As a scriptural prayer which recognizes the evangelical role of Mary, it is the treasure of *all* Christians. It is truly an ecumenical devotion. No one who glories in the name of Christian would oppose the prayerful contemplation of the Gospel, nor would any follower of Jesus refuse to recognize, in a loving manner, the singular role which Mary plays in our redemption as the Mother and Associate of the Redeemer. The Rosary is then a prayer in which all Christians can join. It is heartwarming to learn of the devotion of many of our separated brethren to the prayerful recitation of the Rosary. As the true nature of this Gospel prayer becomes better known, one can expect the Rosary to become more and more a prayer of all Christians.

The Church so strongly promotes the Rosary for still another reason: experience has proven its power to draw the faithful more deeply into the sacramental life of the Church.

This is so evident at the great Marian pilgrimage centers. Where, for example, is the Eucharist celebrated with such devotion and by such multitudes as can be seen at the shrines of Mary? Every day there is a magnificent procession of the Blessed Sacrament at Lourdes, which is truly the eucharistic shrine of the world. Notice how Our Lady of the Rosary is leading the Pilgrim People of God to the adoration of her Son in the Eucharist, to the celebration of the Holy Sacrifice of the Mass. The long line of penitents waiting to celebrate the Sacrament of Reconciliation is characteristic of the great Rosary shrines of Lourdes and Fatima. Again, the Mother is leading her children to the Lord! As Paul VI puts it so forcefully, "Love for the Church will become love for Mary, and vice versa, since one cannot exist without the other" (*On Devotion to the Blessed Virgin Mary*, No. 28).

For our own times, there is another strong motivation for the daily recitation of the Rosary. The two great modern apparitions of Mary, Lourdes and Fatima, earnestly call for the recitation of the Rosary. They ratify all that the Church has said about the beauty and power of the Rosary.

At Fatima especially, Mary's fervent plea calls for the daily recitation of the Rosary, and, on the First Saturdays, the recitation of the Rosary joined with fifteen minutes of meditation. The Fatima requests become so attractive when seen in the light of the nature of the Rosary: a Gospel prayer, outlining the history of our redemption; a contemplative praise of God for the saving mysteries accomplished by Jesus, who is always the Son of Mary.

No wonder that Our Lady told us at Fatima that peace would come about through the Rosary! For in our reciting the Rosary, the power of the Holy Spirit centers us on the Prince of Peace, Jesus the Lord; in our praying the Rosary, the Spirit strengthens us to live the radical demands of the Gospel. The apparitions of Our Lady of Fatima, so cherished by the Church, are a constant reminder of the importance of the Rosary.

Our beloved Holy Father John Paul II, a constant promoter of Marian devotion, beautifully summarized the power of the Rosary and its link to the message of Fatima when he consecrated the world to the Immaculate Heart of Mary on May 13, 1982. In his homily at Fatima on that momentous day, he proclaimed: "The call to repentance is linked, as always, with a call to prayer. In harmony with the tradition of so many centuries, the Lady of the message [of Fatima] indicates the Rosary, which can rightly be defined as "Mary's prayer": the prayer in which she feels particularly united with us. She herself prays with us. The Rosary prayer embraces the problems of the Church, of the See of Saint Peter, the problems of the whole world. In it we also remember sinners, that they may be converted and saved, and the souls in Purgatory."

II

The Prayers
and Practice
of the Rosary

1. *The Rosary Prayers*

The Sign of the Cross

Following the ancient custom of the Church, we seal our prayers, at the beginning and the conclusion, with the Name of the Trinity, as we sign ourselves with the great sign of our salvation, the Cross of our Lord Jesus Christ:

In the Name of the Father, and of the
Son, and of the
Holy Spirit, Amen.

The Apostles' Creed

Holding the crucifix of the Rosary, we begin our prayer with the ancient profession of faith, called the Apostles' Creed:

I believe in God, the Father Almighty, Creator of heaven and earth; and in Jesus Christ, His only Son, Our Lord: Who was conceived by the Holy Spirit, born of the virgin Mary, suffered under Pontius Pilate, was crucified, died and was buried. He descended into hell: the third day He arose again from the dead; He ascended into heaven, sits at the right hand of God, the Father Almighty; from thence He shall come to judge the living and the dead. I believe in the Holy Spirit, the holy Catholic Church, the communion of saints, the forgiveness of sins, the resurrection of the body, and life everlasting. Amen.

The Our Father

We begin each decade of the Rosary with the prayer Our Lord Himself taught us:

Our Father, Who art in heaven, hallowed be Thy Name. Thy kingdom come; Thy will be done on earth, as it is in heaven. Give us this day our daily bread; and forgive us our trespasses as we forgive those who trespass against us. And lead us not into temptation, but deliver us from evil. Amen.

The Hail Mary

As we finger the ten beads of each mystery, we praise Mary with the words of greeting offered to her by the Angel Gabriel and by her cousin Saint Elizabeth; the second part of the prayer dates from the early ages of the Church:

Hail Mary, full of grace, the Lord is with thee; blessed art thou among women and blessed is the fruit of thy womb, Jesus. Holy Mary, Mother of God, pray for us sinners, now and at the hour of our death. Amen.

The Glory Be to the Father

From ancient times, the Church has offered to the Most Blessed Trinity this doxology (meaning, words of glory and praise) as the final verse of each psalm. The praise forms a fitting conclusion of each decade of the Rosary:

Glory be to the Father, and to the Son, and to the Holy Spirit. As it was in the beginning, is now and ever shall be, world without end. Amen.

Optional Concluding Prayers

The beautiful medieval prayer to Our Lady, the Hail Holy Queen (Salve Regina), *is the traditional concluding prayer to the recitation of the Rosary:*

Hail, holy Queen, Mother of mercy; hail our life, our sweetness and our hope. To thee do we cry, poor banished children of Eve. To thee do we send up our sighs, mourning and weeping in this valley of tears. Turn then, most gracious Advocate, thine eyes of mercy toward us. And after this our exile show unto us the blessed fruit of thy womb, Jesus. O clement, O loving, O sweet Virgin Mary.

The following prayer, taken from the Mass of the Feast of the Most Holy Rosary, is also often used as a conclusion to the Rosary:

O God, whose only begotten Son, by His life, death and resurrection, has purchased for us the reward of eternal life; grant, we beseech You, that meditating upon these mysteries of the Most Holy Rosary of the Blessed Virgin Mary, we may imitate what they contain and obtain what they promise. We make this prayer in the Name of Jesus the Lord. Amen.

To which is often added:

May the Divine Assistance remain always with us. And may the souls of the faithful departed, through the mercy of God, rest in peace. Amen.

2. *The Manner of Praying the Rosary*

The Rosary is extremely simple to say, which is one of the reasons for its great popularity among Christians.

The Rosary begins with the *Sign of the Cross.* Then, while holding the Crucifix of the Beads, the *Apostles' Creed* is recited. In a communal celebration, it is well for the leader to begin with the opening sentence of the Creed, *I believe in God,* and then everyone else may join in the profession of faith.

The *Our Father* is prayed on the first bead after the Crucifix. Whenever the *Our Father* is recited in a communal celebration, the leader may recite the first half and the rest of the group may respond with the second half; or half the group may recite the first part of the *Our Father*, the rest of the group, the second part.

Three *Hail Mary's* are recited on the next three small beads. Again, in a communal celebration, the leader may recite the first half of the *Hail Mary* and the others respond; or half the group may recite the first part of the *Hail Mary*, the rest of the group, the second part.

After the three *Hail Mary's*, the *Glory Be to the Father* is recited. Again, the leader or half the group may recite the first part (*Glory be to the Father, and to the Son and to the Holy Spirit*), the rest of the group, the second part of the prayer.

The meditation on the mysteries now begins. The ten beads more closely linked together (and often smaller than the other beads) indicate the recitation of the *Hail Mary*. While fingering the larger bead which separates the sets of ten smaller beads, the *Our Father* is prayed. At the end of every *Our Father*, together with ten *Hail Mary's*, one concludes with the *Glory Be to the Father*.

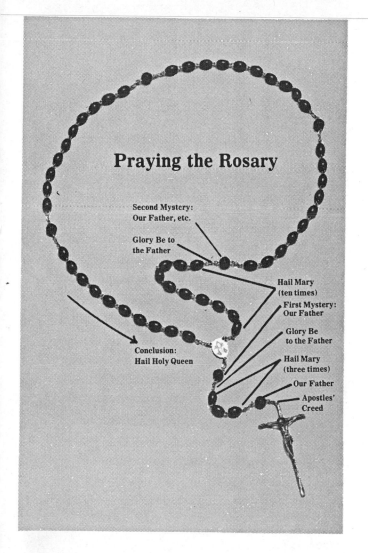

Praying the Rosary

Second Mystery:
Our Father, etc.

Glory Be to
the Father

Hail Mary
(ten times)

First Mystery:
Our Father

Glory Be
to the Father

Hail Mary
(three times)

Our Father

Apostles'
Creed

Conclusion:
Hail Holy Queen

A decade of the Rosary, during which the faithful meditate on one of the Gospel mysteries, consists, therefore, of an *Our Father*, ten *Hail Mary's* and the *Glory Be to the Father*.

Reciting the Rosary daily means praying five decades, that is, either the Joyful, or the Sorrowful, or the Glorious Mysteries, each of which forms a unit in itself. (There are some of the faithful who pray the entire Rosary, that is, the fifteen decades, every day, usually reciting the Joyful Mysteries in the morning, the Sorrowful in the afternoon, and the Glorious in the evening.)

It is the strong wish of the Church, which was so emphasized by Our Lady of Fatima, that all the faithful pray the Rosary (that is, at least five decades) every day.

3. Indulgences for the Recitation of the Rosary

The Enchiridion of Indulgences, Authorized English Edition, published by The Catholic Book Publishing Co., New York (1969), contains the following indulgences granted by the Church for the recitation of the Rosary (that is, five decades):

A *plenary indulgence* is granted, if the Rosary is recited in a church or public oratory or in a family group, a religious community or a pious association; a *partial indulgence* is granted in other circumstances.

III

The Method
of Using
the Rosary
Meditations

The Method of Using the Rosary Meditations

Before entering into the Rosary meditations themselves, it may be well to offer some explanations concerning the method of praying the Rosary which is proposed in this book.

1. Five possible points of meditation are offered for each of the Rosary mysteries. *It is important to note that these are only suggested topics.* Moreover, not all of them need be used; perhaps one or two may suffice. Personal circumstances and also the liturgical season or feast day will dictate how they should be used and how they may be applied to the actual joys and sorrows of one's own personal life.

2. Since the Rosary is a Gospel prayer, a central scriptural reference will be found under the heading of each mystery. Some may prefer to read the text before the recitation of each decade. A brief text from Scripture is usually included with each topic for reflection; it is hoped that this will be an aid in centering thoughts on the Gospel narrative. Instead of a Scripture verse, brief texts from the Second Vatican Council or occasional personal reflections are used for some of the possible points of meditation.

3. The introductory prayers for each Rosary recitation itself, as well as beginning and concluding prayers for each mystery, are adapted from a favorite method of Saint Louis de Montfort as found in his *Admirable Secret of the Most Holy Rosary*. These prayers can be further adapted to respond to one's own personal circumstances. At the conclusion of each mystery, the prayer taught by Our Lady to the three children of Fatima is used. While this has different versions, the version used is the prayer taken from the Memoirs of Lucia, which were published in English, with the Imprimatur of the Bishop of Fatima, on May 13, 1976.

4. The points presented for reflection are sim-

ple and can easily be remembered. This may be a help in reciting the Rosary even when we cannot have this book with us. Although the privileged place of prayer is before the Blessed Sacrament, this is not always possible. Many people find that they can pray the Rosary with great devotion while, for example, riding the bus, or driving to the office, or taking a stroll.

5. Group recitation of the Rosary is strongly encouraged. It is hoped that this book will promote the community recitation of the Rosary, especially within the family. When God's children are gathered together in His holy Name, the Rosary is a beautiful means of praising God and asking for His blessing upon the individuals and upon the group as a whole.

The family especially — and religious communities and priests living together — should find a suitable time of the day when all can gather to reflect on God's saving love through the common recitation of the Rosary. Our Lady, the Mother of us all, binds us together through this communal recitation into one family of love.

6. When the Rosary is recited in a small group, it is well to consider sharing with one an-

other the inspirations of the Spirit. With all simplicity, one or another member of the group may briefly share with the others his or her reflections on the mystery. This is not only a means of praising God and thanking Him for His gifts, but it is also an encouragement to others.

7. Even when a person cannot be physically present with a group, a spiritual bond of union with others may be formed as we recite the Rosary. This can take on many forms. Spiritually, a bond may be made with all the people of a certain locality, or with those who are dying, or with those suffering persecution for the Faith, or with all missionaries, or with all the members of our family.

8. A popular form of prayer is known as the Novena of Rosaries. It consists in saying the Rosary in petition at the beginning of a month for 27 days; for the remainder of the month one says the Rosary for whatever intention one may wish. At the beginning of the second month the Rosary is said in thanksgiving for the request of the preceding month. In this way, a union of prayer may be established between friends who live at a distance. They can be reached by phone or letter

about the intentions they may wish to have remembered.

One final word: concerning distractions during the recitation of the Rosary. In today's hectic
world, distractions appear to be a natural accom-
paniment to prayer! They should not be a source
of disturbance or discouragement. When one no-
tices that the mind is drifting away from the
Gospel mystery, the heart peacefully invokes the
Lord asking for strength to praise Him. Then the
prayer continues.

One of the best antidotes to distractions is to
prepare for prayer. Before entering into recitation of the mysteries of the Rosary, there should
be a few minutes of silence to put aside everything else and slowly become immersed in the
presence of God. Moreover, the praying of the
Rosary should never become rushed. A rapid recitation of the Rosary invites numerous distractions. A place of *quiet* is also an important ingre-
dient in avoiding distractions. Some people can be
in a spirit of deep recollection even while in a
bustling airport; others would find such a place
impossible for the recitation of the Rosary. Each
person, each group, will be able to discover the

best place and the best manner to praise God through the Rosary meditations.

The power of the Rosary is impossible to describe. It must be experienced in order to be believed! The intrinsic beauty of the Rosary will attract us to its daily recitation.

May the Lord bless all who will use this book as a possible aid in praying the Rosary. All who use these meditations truly form a *spiritual community*, supporting one another by the daily Rosary. Through these meditations, one will experience that "the peace of God, which passes all understanding, will keep your hearts and your minds in Christ Jesus" (Phil 4:7).

Novena Record

In Petition

1 J	2 S	3 G	4 J	5 S	6 G	7 J	8 S	9 G
10 J	11 S	12 G	13 J	14 S	15 G	16 J	17 S	18 G
19 J	20 S	21 G	22 J	23 S	24 G	25 J	26 S	27 G

In Thanksgiving

1 J	2 S	3 G	4 J	5 S	6 G	7 J	8 S	9 G
10 J	11 S	12 G	13 J	14 S	15 G	16 J	17 S	18 G
19 J	20 S	21 G	22 J	23 S	24 G	25 J	26 S	27 G

Mysteries of the Rosary

Joyful

1. The Annunciation
2. The Visitation
3. The Nativity
4. The Presentation
5. The Finding in the Temple

Sorrowful

1. The Agony in the Garden
2. The Scourging at the Pillar
3. The Crowning with Thorns
4. The Carrying of the Cross
5. The Crucifixion

Glorious

1. The Resurrection
2. The Ascension
3. The Descent of the Holy Spirit
4. The Assumption
5. The Coronation of Mary

IV

Meditations
on the Mysteries
of the Rosary

Prayer at the Beginning
of the Rosary

I unite with all the saints in heaven, with all the just on earth, with all the faithful here assembled; I unite myself to You, my dear Jesus, in order to praise worthily Your most holy Mother and to praise You in her and through her.

I offer You, O Lord Jesus, this *Creed* in honor of all the Mysteries of our Faith, this *Our Father* and these three *Hail Mary's* in honor of our One God, Father, Son and Holy Spirit. I ask of You a lively faith, a firm hope and an ardent charity.

(Say Apostles' Creed, Our Father, three Hail Mary's, Glory Be.)

The Joyful Mysteries of the Rosary

With Mary and under her maternal influence, may I contemplate the joyful mysteries of Jesus-Emmanuel, as the Holy Spirit describes them especially in the first two chapters of Matthew and Luke.

1. Annunciation of the Lord
(Lk 1:26-38)

I offer You, O Lord Jesus, this first joyful mystery in honor of Your Incarnation in the womb of Mary. I ask of You in this mystery, and through her intercession, the gift of total surrender to Your Love. *(Our Father, ten Hail Mary's.)*

Possible points of meditation:

a) **God Sends the Angel Gabriel to Mary:** "In the sixth month the angel Gabriel was sent from God to a city of Galilee named Nazareth, to a virgin betrothed to a man whose name was Joseph, of the house of David; and the virgin's name was Mary." (Lk 1:26-27)

b) **The Greeting and Message of the Angel Gabriel:** "And He came to her and said, 'Hail, full of grace, the Lord is with you!. . . You will conceive in your womb and bear a son, and you shall call his name Jesus . . . for He will save his people from their sins.' " (Lk 1:28,31; Mt 1:21)

First Joyful Mystery: The Annunciation

c) **Mary Overshadowed by the Holy Spirit:** In response to Mary's concern, the Angel explains: "The Holy Spirit will come upon you, and the power of the Most High will overshadow you; therefore the child to be born will be called holy, the Son of God." (Lk 1:35)

d) **Mary's Total Consent:** "And Mary said, 'Behold, I am the handmaid of the Lord; let it be to me according to your word.' " (Lk 1:38)

e) **The Tremendous Effect of Mary's Surrender:** "And the Word became flesh and dwelt among us, full of grace and truth; we have beheld his glory, glory as of the only Son from the Father." (Jn 1:14)

    The Incarnation is a reality!

At the conclusion of the decade: (Glory Be.)

O my Jesus, forgive us, save us from the fire of hell. Lead all souls to heaven, especially those most in need.

May the grace of the mystery of the Incarnation come into my heart. Amen.

2. The Visitation
(Lk 1:39-56)

I offer You, O Lord Jesus, this second joyful mystery in honor of the Visitation of Your Mother to her cousin Saint Elizabeth. I ask of You in this mystery, and through the intercession of Your most holy Mother, great charity toward others. *(Our Father, ten Hail Mary's.)*

Possible points of meditation:

a) **Mary's Journey to Her Cousin, Saint Elizabeth:** "In those days Mary arose and went with haste into the hill country, to a city of Judah, and she entered the house of Zechariah and greeted Elizabeth." (Lk 1:39-40)

b) **Elizabeth Greets Mary:** "Elizabeth was filled with the Holy Spirit and she exclaimed with a loud cry, 'Blessed are you among women, and blessed is the fruit of your womb!' " (Lk 1:41-42)

Second Joyful Mystery: The Visitation

c) **The Sanctification of John the Baptizer:** "And why is this granted to me, that the mother of my Lord should come to me? For behold, when the voice of your greeting came to my ears, the babe in my womb leaped for joy." (Lk 1:43-44)

d) **Elizabeth's Praise of Mary's Faith:** "And blessed is she who believed that there would be a fulfillment of what was spoken to her from the Lord." (Lk 1:45)

e) **Mary's Song of Praise:** "My soul magnifies the Lord, and my spirit rejoices in God my Savior, for he has regarded the low estate of his handmaiden. For behold, henceforth all generations will call me blessed; for he who is mighty has done great things for me, and holy is his name." (Lk 1:46-49)

At the conclusion of the decade: (Glory Be.)

O my Jesus, forgive us, save us from the fire of hell. Lead all souls to heaven, especially those most in need.

May the grace of the mystery of the Visitation come into my heart. Amen.

3. The Nativity of Our Lord
(Lk 2:1-20)

I offer You, O Lord Jesus, this third joyful mystery in honor of Your Nativity in the stable of Bethlehem. I ask of You in this mystery, and through the intercession of Your most holy Mother, detachment from the things of this world. *(Our Father, ten Hail Mary's.)*

Possible points of meditation:

a) **The Journey to Bethlehem:** "In those days a decree went out from Caesar Augustus that all the world should be enrolled. . . . And Joseph also went up from Galilee, from the city of Nazareth, to Judea, to the city of David, which is called Bethlehem, because he was of the house and lineage of David, to be enrolled with Mary his betrothed, who was with child." (Lk 2:1-5)

b) **The Birth of Jesus:** "And while they were there, the time came for her to be delivered. And she gave birth to her first-born son and

Third Joyful Mystery: The Nativity

wrapped him in swaddling cloths, and laid him in a manger, because there was no place for them in the inn." (Lk 2:6-7)

c) **The Song of the Angels:** "Be not afraid; for behold, I bring you good news of a great joy which shall come to all the people; for to you is born this day in the city of David a Savior, who is Christ the Lord. . . ." And suddenly there was with the angel a multitude of the heavenly host praising God and saying: 'Glory to God in the highest / and on earth peace among men with whom he is pleased!' " (Lk 2:10-14)

d) **The Adoration of the Shepherds:** "The shepherds said to one another: 'Let us go over to Bethlehem and see this thing that has happened, which the Lord has made known to us.' And they went with haste, and found Mary and Joseph, and the babe lying in a manger." (Lk 2:15-16)

e) **The Adoration of the Wise Men:** "When they saw the star, they rejoiced exceedingly with great joy. . . . and they fell and worshipped him. Then, opening their treasures, they offered him gifts, gold and frankincense and myrrh. . . . But Mary kept all these things, pondering them in her heart." (Mt 2:10-11; Lk 2:19)

At the conclusion of the decade: (Glory Be.)

O my Jesus, forgive us, save us from the fire of hell. Lead all souls to heaven, especially those most in need.

May the grace of the mystery of the Nativity come into my heart. Amen.

Fourth Joyful Mystery: The Presentation

4. The Presentation of the Lord
(Lk 2:22-38)

I offer You, O Lord Jesus, this fourth joyful mystery in honor of Your Presentation in the Temple, and I ask of You in this mystery, and through the intercession of Your most holy Mother, great purity of body and soul. *(Our Father, ten Hail Mary's.)*

Possible points of meditation:

a) **The Obedience of Joseph and Mary:** "And when the time came for their purification according to the law of Moses, they brought him up to Jerusalem to present him to the Lord. . . ." (Lk 2:22)

b) **The Praise Offered by Simeon:** "And when the parents brought in the child Jesus, to do for him according to the custom of the law, he took him up in his arms and blessed God and said, 'Lord, now lettest thou thy servant depart in peace according to thy word; for

63

mine eyes have seen thy salvation . . . a light for revelation to the Gentiles, and for the glory of thy people Israel.' " (Lk 2:27-32)

c) **Simeon's Prophecy:** "And his father and his mother marveled at what was said about him. And Simeon blessed them and said to Mary his mother. . . . 'And a sword shall pierce through your soul also. . . .' " (Lk 2:33-35)

d) **The Praise Offered by Anna:** "And there was a prophetess, Anna. . . . ; she was of great age. . . . she did not depart from the temple, worshiping with fasting and prayer night and day. And coming up at that very hour she gave thanks to God, and spoke of him to all who were looking for the redemption of Jerusalem." (Lk 2:36-38)

e) **The Return to Nazareth:** "And when they had performed everything according to the law of the Lord, they returned into Galilee, to their own city, Nazareth. And the child grew and became strong, filled with wisdom; and the favor of God was upon him." (Lk 2:39-40)

At the conclusion of the decade: (Glory Be.)

O My Jesus, forgive us, save us from the fire of hell. Lead all the souls to heaven, especially those most in need.

May the grace of the mystery of the Presentation come into my heart. Amen.

5. The Finding of Jesus in the Temple
(Lk 2:41-52)

I offer You, O Lord Jesus, this fifth joyful mystery in honor of the finding in the temple, and I ask of You in this mystery, and through the intercession of Your most holy Mother, the gift of true wisdom. *(Our Father, ten Hail Mary's.)*

Possible points of meditation:

a) **The Journey to Jerusalem:** "Now his parents went to Jerusalem every year at the feast of the Passover. And when he was twelve years old, they went up according to custom." (Lk 2:41-42)

b) **The Loss of Jesus:** "The boy Jesus stayed behind in Jerusalem. His parents did not know it . . . and when they did not find him, they returned to Jerusalem, seeking him." (Lk 2:43-45)

c) **The Finding of Jesus:** "After three days, they found him in the temple, sitting among the

Fifth Joyful Mystery: The Finding in the Temple

teachers, listening to them and asking them questions; and all who heard him were amazed at his understanding and his answers." (Lk 2:46-47)

d) The Questioning by Mary: "His mother said to him: 'Son, why have you treated us so? Behold, your father and I have been looking for you anxiously.' And he said to them: 'How is it that you sought me? Did you not know that I must be in my Father's house?' " (Lk 2:48-49)

e) The Wonderment of Joseph and Mary: "And they did not understand the saying which he spoke to them. And he went down with them and came to Nazareth, and was obedient to them; and his mother kept all these things in her heart." (Lk 2:50-51)

At the conclusion of the decade: (Glory Be.)

O My Jesus, forgive us, save us from the fire of hell. Lead all souls to heaven especially those most in need.

May the grace of the mystery of the Finding in the Temple come into my heart. Amen.

The Sorrowful Mysteries of the Rosary

With Mary and under her maternal influence, may I contemplate the sorrowful mysteries of Jesus, Suffering Savior, as the Holy Spirit describes them especially in the passion narratives of the Gospels.

1. The Agony in the Garden
(Lk 22:39-46)

I offer You, O Lord Jesus, this first sorrowful mystery in honor of Your Agony in the Garden. I ask of You in this mystery, and through the intercession of Your most holy Mother, contrition for my sins. *(Our Father, ten Hail Mary's.)*

Possible points of meditation:

a) **Jesus Goes to Gethsemane to Pray:** "And they went to a place which was called Gethsemane; and he said to his disciples, 'Sit here, while I pray.' " (Mk 14:32)

b) **The Prayer of Resignation of Jesus to the Father:** "And he said, 'Abba, Father, all things are possible to thee; remove this cup from me; yet not what I will, but what thou wilt.' " (Mk 14:36)

c) **The Agony of Jesus:** "And being in an agony he prayed more earnestly; and his sweat be-

First Sorrowful Mystery: The Agony in the Garden

came like great drops of blood falling down upon the ground." (Lk 22:44)

d) The Call of Jesus to Watch and Pray: "Watch and Pray that you may not enter into temptation; the spirit indeed is willing but the flesh is weak." (Mt 26:41)

e) The Weakness of the Disciples: "And he came the third time, and said to them, 'Are you still sleeping and taking your rest? It is enough; the hour has come; the Son of man is betrayed into the hands of sinners. Rise, let us be going; see, my betrayer is at hand.' " (Mk 14:41-42)

At the conclusion of the decade: (Glory Be.)

O my Jesus, forgive us, save us from the fire of hell. Lead all souls to heaven, especially those most in need.

May the grace of the mystery of the Agony in the Garden come into my heart. Amen.

2. The Scourging at the Pillar
(Lk 23:1-25)

I offer You, O Lord Jesus, this second sorrowful mystery in honor of Your bloody scourging at the pillar, and I ask of You in this mystery, and through the intercession of Your most holy Mother, the spirit of mortification. *(Our Father, ten Hail Mary's.)*

Possible points of meditation:

a) **The Interrogation by Pilate:** After having been condemned by the Sanhedrin, Jesus is brought before the Roman Governor, Pontius Pilate, who alone was authorized to pass the death sentence: "Pilate entered the praetorium again and called Jesus and said to him, 'Are you the King of the Jews? . . . Where are you from? . . . Do you not know that I have the power to release you, and the

Second Sorrowful Mystery: The Scourging at the Pillar.

power to crucify you?' " (Jn 18:33;19:9-10)

b) **The Response of Jesus:** "My kingship is not of this world; if my kingship were of this world, my servants would fight that I might not be handed over to the Jews; but my kingship is not from the world." (Jn 18:36)

c) **The Verdict of Pilate:** " 'What evil has he done? I have found in him no crime deserving of death; I will therefore chastise him and release him.' [And Pilate then had Jesus taken away and scourged.] But they were urgent, demanding with loud cries that he should be crucified. . . . So Pilate gave sentence that their demand should be granted." (Lk 23:22-24)

d) **Jesus Is Scourged:** "And some began to spit on him, and to cover his face, and to strike him, saying to him, 'Prophesy!' And the guards received him with blows." (Mk 14:65)

e) **Jesus, the Suffering Servant:** "He was wounded for our transgressions, he was bruised for our iniquities; upon him was the chastisement that made us whole, and with

79

his stripes we are healed." (Is 53:5)

At the conclusion of the decade: (Glory Be.)

O My Jesus, forgive us, save us from the fire of hell. Lead all souls to heaven, especially those most in need.

May the grace of the mystery of the scourging at the pillar come into my heart. Amen.

Third Sorrowful Mystery: The Crowning with Thorns

3. The Crowning With Thorns
(Mk 15:16-20)

I offer you, O Lord Jesus, this third sorrowful mystery in honor of Your crowning with thorns, and I ask of You in this mystery, and through the intercession of Your most holy Mother, the strength to live for You alone. *(Our Father, ten Hail Mary's.)*

Possible points of meditation:

a) **Jesus Predicts His Passion:** "And [Jesus] began to teach them that the Son of Man must suffer many things, and be rejected by the elders and the chief priests and the scribes, and be killed. . . ." (Mk 8:31)

b) **Jesus Crowned with Thorns:** "And the soldiers plaited a crown of thorns and put it on his head, and arrayed him in a purple robe; they

83

came up to him, saying, 'Hail, King of the Jews!' and struck him with their hands." (Jn 19:2-3)

c) **Jesus Stripped of His Garments:** "And they stripped him and put a scarlet robe upon him . . . and put a reed in his right hand. . . . And they spat upon him, and took a reed and struck him on the head. And when they had mocked him, they stripped him of his robe, and put his clothes on him." (Mt 27:28-31)

d) **Barabbas Preferred to Jesus:** "[Pilate] told them, '. . . You have a custom that I should release one man for you at the Passover; will you have me release for you the King of the Jews?' They cried out again, 'Not this man, but Barabbas!' Now Barabbas was a robber." (Jn 18:39-40)

e) **The Voice of the People: Crucify Him!** "And Pilate again said to them, 'Then what shall I do with the man whom you call the King of the Jews?' And they cried out again, 'Crucify him.' . . . They shouted all the more, 'Crucify him.' " (Mk 15:12-14)

At the end of the decade: (Glory Be.)

O My Jesus, forgive us, save us from the fire of hell. Lead all souls to heaven, especially those most in need.

May the grace of the mystery of the Crowning with Thorns come into my heart. Amen.

4. The Carrying of the Cross
(Lk 23:26-32)

I offer You, O Lord Jesus, this fourth sorrowful mystery in honor of Your carrying of Your
cross, and I ask of You in this mystery, and
through the intercession of Your most holy Mother, the grace to bear my cross patiently. *(Our
Father, ten Hail Mary's.)*

Possible points of meditation:

a) **Jesus Carries His Cross:** "So they took Jesus,
   and he went out, bearing his own cross, to
   the place called the place of a skull, which is
   called in Hebrew Golgotha." (Jn 19:17)

b) **Jesus Meets His Sorrowful Mother:** Scripture
   tells us that Mary stood by the Cross of her
   Son; it has always been the pious belief of
   the faithful that she was with Him during
   His Way of the Cross, bravely following him
   to the hill of Calvary. Who could ever describe the loving, painful emotions of their
   hearts as Mother and Son gaze at each other

Fourth Sorrowful Mystery: The Carrying of the Cross

as He bears His Cross to the skull hill?

c) **Simon of Cyrene Aids Jesus:** "And they compelled a passer-by, Simon of Cyrene, who was coming from the country . . . to carry his cross." (Mk 15:21)

d) **Jesus Consoles the Women of Jerusalem:** "Daughters of Jerusalem, do not weep for me, but weep for yourselves and for your children." (Lk 23:28)

e) **Jesus, Carrying the Sins of the World:** "The Lord has laid on him the iniquity of us all. He was oppressed, and he was afflicted, yet he opened not his mouth; like a lamb that is led to the slaughter, and like a sheep that before its shearers is dumb, so he opened not his mouth." (Is 53:6-7)

At the end of the decade: (Glory Be.)

O My Jesus, forgive us, save us from the fire of hell. Lead all souls to heaven, especially those most in need.

May the grace of the mystery of the Carrying of the Cross come into my heart. Amen.

5. The Crucifixion of Jesus
(Jn 19:17-30)

I offer You, O Lord Jesus, this fifth sorrowful mystery in honor of Your crucifixion and ignominious death on Calvary. I ask of You in this mystery, and through the intercession of Your most holy Mother, the conversion of sinners and the perseverance of the just. *(Our Father, ten Hail Mary's.)*

Possible points of meditation:

a) **Jesus Is Nailed to the Cross:** "And they brought him to the place called Golgotha (which means the place of a skull). And they offered him wine mingled with myrrh; but he did not take it. And they crucified him. . . ." (Mk 15:22-23)

b) **Hanging from the Cross, Jesus Forgives His**

Fifth Sorrowful Mystery: The Crucifixion

Persecutors: "And when they came to the place which is called The Skull, there they crucified him, and the criminals, one on the right and one on the left. And Jesus said, 'Father, forgive them; for they know not what they do.' " (Lk 23:33-34)

c) **Jesus Promises Paradise to the Penitent Thief:** (One of the criminals hanging on the cross next to Jesus said to Him:) " 'Jesus, remember me when you come in your kingly power.' And he said to him, 'Truly, I say to you, today you will be with me in Paradise.' " (Lk 23:42-43)

d) **Jesus Gives Us Mary as Our Mother:** "When Jesus saw his mother, and the disciple whom he loved standing near, he said to his mother, 'Woman, behold, your son!' Then he said to the disciple, 'Behold, your mother!' " (Jn 19:26)

e) **Jesus Dies upon the Cross:** "And when the sixth hour had come, there was darkness over the whole land until the ninth hour. And at the ninth hour Jesus cried with a loud voice, '. . . My God, my God, why has thou forsaken me?'. . . And Jesus uttered a loud cry, and breathed his last.'' (Mk 15:33-37)

At the conclusion of the decade: (Glory Be.)

O My Jesus, forgive us, save us from the fire of hell. Lead all souls to heaven, especially those most in need.

May the grace of the mystery of the Crucifixion come into my heart. Amen.

The Glorious Mysteries of the Rosary

With Mary and under her maternal influence, may I contemplate the glorious mysteries of Jesus, Risen Lord, as the Holy Spirit describes them especially in the Easter narratives of the Gospels.

1. The Resurrection
(Jn 20:1-31)

I offer You, O Lord Jesus, this first glorious mystery in honor of Your Resurrection from the dead. I ask of You in this mystery, and through the intercession of Your most holy Mother, love of God and fervor in Your service. *(Our Father, ten Hail Mary's.)*

Possible points of meditation:

a) **The Burial of Jesus:** "And [Joseph of Arimathea] bought a linen shroud, and taking him down, wrapped him in the linen shroud, and laid him in a tomb which had been hewn out of the rock; and he rolled a stone against the door of the tomb." (Mk 15:46)

b) **The Posting of Guards at the Tomb:** "The chief priests and the Pharisees gathered

First Glorious Mystery: The Resurrection

before Pilate and said, 'Sir, we remember how that impostor said, while he was still alive, "After three days I will rise again." Therefore order the sepulchre to be made secure until the third day. . . .' Pilate said to them, 'You have a guard of soldiers; go, make it as secure as you can.' '' (Mt 27:62-65)

c) **The Women at the Tomb:** "Now after the sabbath, toward the dawn of the first day of the week, Mary Magdalene and the other Mary went to see the sepulchre. And behold, there was a great earthquake; for an angel of the Lord descended from heaven and came and rolled back the stone, and sat upon it. His appearance was as lightning, and his raiment white as snow." (Mt 28:1-3)

d) **The Proclamation of the Resurrection:** "The angel said to the women: 'Do not be afraid, for I know that you seek Jesus who was crucified. He is not here; for he has risen as he said. Come, see the place where he lay. Then go quickly and tell his disciples that he has risen from the dead, and behold, he is going before you to Galilee; there you will see him.' '' (Mt 28:5-7)

e) Mary Magdalene Meets Jesus at the Tomb:
"Mary stood weeping outside the tomb . . . she turned around and saw Jesus standing, but she did not know that it was Jesus. Jesus said to her: 'Woman, why are you weeping? Whom do you seek?'. . . Jesus said to her, 'Mary.' She turned and said to him in Hebrew, 'Rabboni!' (which means Teacher)." (Jn 20:11-16)

At the conclusion of the decade: (Glory Be.)

O my Jesus, forgive us, save us from the fire of hell. Lead all souls to heaven especially those most in need.

May the grace of the mystery of the Resurrection come into my heart. Amen.

Second Glorious Mystery: The Ascension

2. The Ascension of the Lord
(Lk 24:44-53)

I offer You, O Lord Jesus, this second glorious
mystery in honor of Your triumphant ascension
into heaven. I ask of You in this mystery, and
through the intercession of Your most loving
mother, an ardent desire for heaven, my true
home. *(Our Father, ten Hail Mary's.)*

Possible points of meditation:

a) **The Risen Lord Appears During Forty Days:**
   "To the apostles he presented himself alive
   after his passion by many proofs, appearing
   to them during forty days, and speaking of
   the kingdom of God." (Acts 1:3)

b) **Jesus Appears to the Doubting Thomas:** "The
   doors were shut, but Jesus came and stood
   among them, and said, 'Peace be to you.'

103

Then he said to Thomas, 'Put your finger here, and see my hands; and put out your hand and place it in my side; do not be faithless, but believing.' Thomas answered him, 'My Lord and my God!' " (Jn 20:26-28)

c) **Jesus Announces His Ascension to the Father:** "Do not hold me, for I have not yet ascended to the Father; but go to my brethren and say to them, I am ascending to my Father and your Father, to my God and your God." (Jn 20:17)

d) **The Great Mandate of the Lord at the Ascension:** "All authority in heaven and on earth has been given to me. Go therefore and make disciples of all nations, baptizing them in the name of the Father and of the Son and of the Holy Spirit, teaching them to observe all that I have commanded you; and so, I am with you always, to the close of the age." (Mt 28:18-20)

e) **The Final Easter Appearance of Jesus to the Apostles:** "Then he led them out as far as Bethany, and lifting up his hands he blessed them. While he blessed them, he parted from them and was carried up into heaven." (Lk 24:50-51)

At the conclusion of the decade: (Glory Be.)

O my Jesus, forgive us, save us from the fire of hell. Lead all souls to heaven especially those most in need.

May the grace of the mystery of the Ascension come into my heart. Amen.

3. The Descent of the Holy Spirit
(Acts 2:1-4)

I offer You, O Lord Jesus, this third glorious mystery in honor of the mystery of Pentecost. I ask of You in this mystery, and through the intercession of Your most holy Mother, the descent of the Holy Spirit into my soul. *(Our Father, ten Hail Mary's.)*

Possible points of meditation:

a) **Jesus Promises to Send the Spirit:** "When the Counselor comes, whom I shall send to you from the Father, even the Spirit of truth, who proceeds from the Father, he will bear witness to me." (Jn 15:26)

b) **The Disciples with Mary in the Upper Room:** "They went into the upper room, where they were staying . . . all these with one accord devoted themselves to prayer, together with

Third Glorious Mystery: The Descent of the Holy Spirit

the women and Mary the mother of Jesus, and with his brethren." (Acts 1:13-14)

c) **The Coming of the Holy Spirit:** "And suddenly a sound came from heaven like the rush of a mighty wind, and it filled all the house where they were sitting. And there appeared to them tongues as of fire, distributed and resting on each one of them. And they were all filled with the Holy Spirit. . . ." (Acts 2:2-4)

d) **The Bold Preaching of the Apostles:** "And when they had prayed, the place in which they were gathered together was shaken; and they were all filled with the Holy Spirit and spoke the word of God with boldness." (Acts 4:13)

e) **Peter's First Sermon and Its Marvelous Results:** "But Peter, standing with the eleven, lifted up his voice and addressed them. . . . Those who received his [Peter's] word were baptized. and there were added that day about three thousand souls. And they devoted themselves to the apostles' teaching and fellowship, to the breaking of bread and the prayers." (Acts 2:14,41-42)

At the conclusion of the decade: (Glory Be.)

O my Jesus, forgive us, save us from the fire of hell. Lead all souls to heaven especially those most in need.

May the grace of the mystery of Pentecost come into my heart. Amen.

Fourth Glorious Mystery: The Assumption

4. The Assumption of Our Blessed Mother
(cf Lk 1:28; cf Vatican Council II, Constitution on the Church, No. 59)

I offer You, O Lord Jesus, this fourth glorious mystery in honor of the Assumption of Mary into heaven. I ask of You in this mystery, and through her intercession, a tender devotion for so good a Mother. *(Our Father, ten Hail Mary's.)*

Possible points of meditation:

a) **Mary Shares in the Victory of Her Son:** "The Lord God said to the serpent, '. . . I will put enmity between you and the woman, and between your seed and her seed; he shall bruise your head, and you shall bruise his heel.' " (Gen 3:15)

b) **Mary Taken Up into Glory:** "The Immaculate Virgin, preserved free from all stain of original sin, was taken up body and soul into heavenly glory when her earthly life was over." (Vatican Council II, Constitution on the Church, No. 59, referring to Pope Pius XII's Encyclical on the Assumption)

c) **Mary, the Image of the Church:** "The Mother of Jesus in the glory which she possesses in body and soul in heaven is the image and the beginning of the Church as it is to be perfected in the world to come." (Vatican Council II, Constitution on the Church, No. 68)

d) **Mary, the Mother of the Church:** "The motherhood of Mary in the order of grace continues uninterruptedly from the consent which she loyally gave at the Annunciation and which she sustained without wavering beneath the cross, until the eternal fulfillment of all the elect." (Vatican Council II, Constitution on the Church, No. 62)

e) **Mary, Sign of Sure Hope:** "Mary shines forth on earth, until the day of the Lord shall come, a sign of certain hope and comfort to the pilgrim people of God." (Vatican Council II, Constitution on the Church, No. 68)

At the conclusion of the decade: (Glory Be.)

O my Jesus, forgive us, save us from the fire of hell. Lead all souls to heaven especially those most in need.

May the grace of the mystery of the Assumption come into my heart. Amen.

5. The Coronation of Mary
(Cf Rev 12:1; Vatican Council II, Constitution on the Church, No. 59)

I offer You, O Lord Jesus, this fifth glorious mystery in honor of the Coronation of Your Mother. I ask of You in this mystery and through her intercession, perseverance in grace and the crown of glory hereafter. *(Our Father, ten Hail Mary's.)*

Possible points of meditation:

a) **Mary Crowned as Queen:** "And a great portent appeared in heaven, a woman clothed with the sun, with the moon under her feet, and on her head a crown of twelve stars." (Rev 12:1)

b) **Mary, the Glory of Our Race:** "You are the exaltation of Jerusalem, you are the great glory of Israel, you are the great pride of our

Fifth Glorious Mystery: The Coronation of Mary

nation! (Jud 15:9) Mary inspires us.

c) **The Love of Mary for Us, Her Children:** "By her eternal charity, she cares for the brethren of her Son, who still journey on earth surrounded by dangers and difficulties, until they are led into their blessed home." (Vatican Council II, Constitution on the Church, No. 62)

d) **Devotion of the People of God to Mary Our Queen:** "Devotion of the People of God towards Mary, in veneration and love, in invocation and imitation, [is] according to her own prophetic words: 'all generations shall call me blessed; for he who is mighty has done great things to me.' " (Vatican Council II, Constitution on the Church No. 66, quoting Lk 1:48)

e) **Mary's Eternal Adoration of Christ the King:** "And [they] worshipped God, saying, "Amen! Blessing and glory and wisdom and thanksgiving and honor and power and might be to our God for ever and ever! Amen." (Rev 7:11-12)

At the conclusion of the decade: (Glory Be.)

O my Jesus, forgive us, save us from the fire of hell. Lead all souls to heaven especially those most in need.

May the grace of the mystery of the Coronation of Mary come into my heart. Amen.